The Story of Ahikar

By Ahiqar

Copyright © 2021 Lamp of Trismegistus. All rights reserved. No part of this publication may be reproduced or transmitted in any form or by any means, electronic or mechanical, including photocopying, recording, or by any information storage and retrieval system, without permission in writing from Lamp of Trismegistus. Reviewers may quote brief passages.

ISBN: 978-1-63118-561-8

Christian Apocrypha Series

Other Books in this Series and Related Titles

The Book of Wisdom of Solomon by King Solomon (978-1-63118-502-1)

The Apocalypse of Peter by Peter (978-1-63118-527-4)

The Gospel of the Nativity of Mary by St. Matthew (978-1-63118-448-2)

The Vision of Saint Paul the Apostle by Paul (978-1-63118-526-7)

Early Translation of the Acts of the Apostles by Luke (978-1-63118-521-2)

The Hymn of Jesus by G. R. S. Mead (978-1-63118-409-3)

Psalms of Solomon by King Solomon (978-1-63118-439-0)

The First and Second Gospels of the Infancy of Jesus Christ (978-1-63118-415-4)

The Book of Parables by Enoch (978-1-63118-429-1)

The Testament of Abraham by Abraham (978-1-63118-441-3)

The Lives of Adam and Eve by Moses (978-1-63118-414-7)

Masonic Symbolism of King Solomon's Temple by A Mackey &c (978-1-63118-442-0)

The Secrets of Enoch by Enoch (978-1-63118-449-9)

Lost Chapters of the Book of Daniel and Related Writings (978-1-63118-417-8)

The Testament of Moses by Moses (978-1-63118-440-6)

The Book of the Watchers by Enoch (978-1-63118-416-1)

Fourth Book of Maccabees by Josephus (978-1-63118-562-5)

The Odes of Solomon by King Solomon (978-1-63118-503-8)

Book of Dreams by Enoch (978-1-63118-437-6)

The Hymns of Hermes by G. R. S. Mead (978-1-63118-405-5)

The Book of Astronomical Secrets by Enoch (978-1-63118-443-7)

Audio Versions are also Available on Audible, Amazon and Apple

Other Books in this Series and Related Titles

The Hidden Mysteries of Christianity by Annie Besant (978–1–63118–534–2)

Rosicrucian Rules, Secret Signs, Codes and Symbols by various (978-1-63118-488-8)

History and Teachings of the Rosicrucians by W W Westcott &c (978-1-63118-487-1)

Freemasonry and the Egyptian Mysteries by C. W. Leadbeater (978-1-63118-456-7)

The Sepher Yetzirah and the Qabalah by M P Hall (978-1-63118-481-9)

Love and Death by Sri Aurobindo (978-1-63118-557-1)

The Historic, Mythic and Mystic Christ by Annie Besant (978–1–63118–533–5)

Masonic and Rosicrucian History by M P Hall & H Voorhis (978-1-63118-486-4)

Some Deeper Aspects of Masonic Symbolism by A E Waite (978-1-63118-461-1)

The Crest-Jewel of Wisdom by Adi Shankara (978-1-63118-475-8)

The Old Past Master by Carl H Claudy (978-1-63118-464-2)

The Influence of Pythagoras on Freemasonry and Other Essays (978-1-63118-404-8)

The Mysteries of Freemasonry & the Druids by various (978-1-63118-444-4)

Buddhist Psalms by Shinran (978-1-63118-465-9)

Catholicism, Yoga and Hinduism by Hartmann &c (978-1-63118-478-9)

Masonic Symbolism of Easter and the Christ in Masonry (978-1-63118-434-5)

Tao Te Ching & Commentary by Lao Tzu & C Johnston (978-1-63118-495-6)

Ancient Mysteries and Secret Societies by M P Hall (978-1-63118-410-9)

The Golden Verses of Pythagoras: Five Translations (978-1-63118-479-6)

Freemasonry & Catholicism by Max Heindel (978-1-63118-508-3)

A Few Masonic Sermons by A. C. Ward &c (978-1-63118-435-2)

Audio versions are also available on Audible, Amazon and Apple

Table of Contents

Series Introduction…7

Introduction…9

Chapter I…11

Chapter II…15

Chapter III…25

Chapter IV…35

Chapter V…41

Chapter VI…51

Chapter VII…59

SERIES INTRODUCTION

The Apocrypha are a loosely knit series of books, written by early vanguards of Christianity (covering the eras of both the old and new testaments), and which comprise somewhere between about a dozen to several hundred titles, depending on whom you ask and how that person defines "Apocrypha." A small selection of these can still be found included in the Catholic bible, while a majority of the books in question, were abandoned by church officials in the early centuries of Christianity. Many of these apocryphal books were originally considered canon by early followers of Christ, in the first four centuries following his birth. It wasn't until the meeting of the Council of Nicaea in 325, that Emperor Constantine and a group of roughly 300 church bishops, gathered together with the goal of defining, standardizing and unifying an otherwise splintering Christianity, that many of these writings ceased to be included in the newly established canon. Enjoy then, this book as an example, of just one of the many books of the Christian Apocrypha, and be sure to check out other titles in this series.

INTRODUCTION

We have in The Story of Ahikar one of the most ancient sources of human thought and wisdom. Its influence can be traced through the legends of many people, including the Koran, and the Old and New Testaments.

A mosaic found in Treves, Germany, pictured among the wise men of the world the character of Ahikar. Here is his colorful tale.

The date of this story has been a subject of lively discussion. Scholars finally put it down about the First Century when they were proved in error by the original story turning up in an Aramaic papyrus of 500 B. C. among the ruins of Elephantine.

The story is obviously fiction and not history. In fact the reader can make its acquaintance in the supplementary pages of *The Arabian Nights*. It is brilliantly written, and the narrative which is full of action, intrigue, and narrow escape holds the attention to the last. The liberty of imagination is the most precious possession of the writer.

The writing divides itself into four phases: (1) The Narrative; (2) The Teaching (a remarkable series of Proverbs); (3) The Journey to Egypt; (4) The Similitudes or Parables (with which Ahikar completes the education of his erring nephew).

CHAPTER I

Ahikar, Grand Vizier of Assyria, has 60 wives but is fated to have no son. Therefore he adopts his nephew. He crams him full of wisdom and knowledge more than of bread and water.

The story of Haiqâr the Wise, Vizier of Sennacherib the King, and of Nadan, sister's son to Haiqâr the Sage.

2 There was a Vizier in the days of King Sennacherib, son of Sarhadum, King of Assyria and Nineveh, a wise man named Haiqâr, and he was Vizier of the king Sennacherib.

3 He had a fine, fortune and much goods, and he was skilful, wise, a philosopher, in knowledge, in opinion and in government, and he had married sixty women, and had built a castle for each of them.

4 But with it all he had no child by any. of these women, who might be his heir.

5 And he was very sad on account of this, and one day he assembled the astrologers and the learned men and the wizards and explained to them his condition and the matter of his barrenness.

6 And they said to him, 'Go, sacrifice to the gods and beseech them that perchance they may provide thee with a boy.'

7 And he did as they told him and offered sacrifices to the idols, and besought them and implored them with request, and entreaty.

8 And they answered him not one word. And he went away sorrowful and dejected, departing with a pain at his heart.

9 And he returned, and implored the Most High God, and believed, beseeching Him with a burning in his heart, saying, 'O Most High God, O Creator of the Heavens and of the earth, O Creator of all created things!

10 I beseech Thee to give me a boy, that I may be consoled by him that he may be present at my heath, that he may close my eyes, and that he may bury me.'

11 Then there came to him a voice saying, 'Inasmuch as thou hast relied first of all on graven images, and hast offered sacrifices to them, for this reason thou shalt remain childless thy life long.

12 But take Nadan thy sister's son, and make him thy child and teach him thy learning and thy good breeding, and at thy death he shall bury thee.'

13 Thereupon he took Nadan his sister's son, who was a little suckling. And he handed him over to eight wet-nurses, that they might suckle him and bring him up.

14 And they brought him up with good food and gentle training and silken clothing, and purple and crimson. And he was seated upon couches of silk.

15 And when Nadan grew big and walked, shooting up like a tall cedar, he taught him good manners and writing and science and philosophy.

16 And after many days King Sennacherib looked at Haiqâr and saw that he had grown very old, and moreover he said to him.

17 'O my honoured friend, the skilful, the trusty, the wise, the governor, my secretary, my vizier, my Chancellor and director; verily thou art grown very old and weighted with years; and thy departure from this world must be near.

18 Tell me who shall have a place in my service after thee.' And Haiqâr said to him, 'O my lord, may thy head live for ever! There is Nadan my sister's son, I have made him my child.

19 And I have brought him up and taught him my wisdom and my knowledge.'

20 And the king said to him, 'O Haiqâr! bring him to my presence, that I may see him, and if I find him suitable, put him in thy place; and thou shalt go thy way, to take a rest and to live the remainder of thy life in sweet repose.'

21 Then Haiqâr went and presented Nadan his sister's son. And he did homage and wished him power and honour.

22 And he looked at him and admired him and rejoiced in him and said to Haiqâr: 'Is this thy son, O Haiqâr? I pray that God may preserve him. And as thou hast served me and my father Sarhadum so may this boy of thine serve me and fulfil my undertakings, my needs, and my business, so that I may honour him and make him powerful for thy sake.'

23 And Haiqâr did obeisance to the king and said to him, 'May thy head live, O my lord the king, for ever! I seek from thee that

thou mayst be patient with my boy Nadan and forgive his mistakes that he may serve thee as it is fitting.'

24 Then the king swore to him that he would make him the greatest of his favourites, and the most powerful of his friends, and that he should be with him in all honour and respect. And he kissed his hands and bade him farewell.

25 And he took Nadan. his sister's son with him and seated him in a parlour and set about teaching him night and day till he had crammed him with wisdom and knowledge more than with bread and water.

CHAPTER II

A "Poor Richard's Almanac" of ancient days. Immortal precepts of human conduct concerning money, women, dress, business, friends. Especially interesting proverbs are found in Verses 12, 17, 23, 37, 45, 47. Compare Verse 63 with some of the cynicism of today.

Thus he taught him, saying: 'O my son! hear my speech and follow my advice and remember what I say.

2 O my son! if thou hearest a word, let it die in thy heart, and reveal it not to another, lest it become a live coal and burn thy tongue and cause a pain in thy body, and thou gain a reproach, and art shamed before God and man.

3 O my son! if thou hast heard a report, spread it not; and if thou hast seen something, tell it not.

4 O my son! make thy eloquence easy to the listener, and be not hasty to return an answer.

5 O my son! when thou hast heard anything, hide it not.

6 O my son! loose not a sealed knot, nor untie it, and seal not a loosened knot.

7 O my son! covet not outward beauty, for it wanes and passes away, but an honourable remembrance lasts for aye.

8 O my son! let not a silly woman deceive thee with her speech, lest thou die the most miserable of deaths, and she entangle thee in the net till thou art ensnared.

9 O my son! desire not a woman bedizened with dress and with ointments, who is despicable and silly in her soul. Woe o thee if thou bestow on her anything that is thine, or commit to her what is in thine hand and she entice thee into sin, and God be wroth with thee.

10 O my son! be not like the almond-tree, for it brings forth leaves before all the trees, and edible fruit after them all, but be like the mulberry-tree, which brings forth edible fruit before all the trees, and leaves after them all.

11 O my son! bend thy head low down, and soften thy voice, and be courteous, and walk in the straight path, and be not foolish. And raise not thy voice when thou laughest for if it were by a loud voice that a house was built, the ass would build many houses every day; and if it were by dint of strength that the plough were driven, the plough would never be removed from under the shoulders of the camels.

12 O m son! the removing of stones with a wise man is better than the drinking of wine with a sorry man.

13 O my son! pour out thy wine on the tombs of the just, and drink not with ignorant, contemptible people.

14 O my son! cleave to wise men who fear God and be like them, and go not near the ignorant, lest thou become like him and learn his ways.

15 O my son! when thou hast got thee a comrade or a friend, try him, and afterwards make him a comrade and a friend; and do

not praise him without a trial; and do not spoil thy speech with a man who lacks wisdom.

16 O my son! while a shoe stays on thy foot, walk with it on the thorns, and make a road for thy son, and for thy household and thy children, and make thy ship taut before she goes on the sea and its waves and sinks and cannot be saved.

17 O my son! if the rich man eat a snake, they say,--"It is by his wisdom," and if a poor man eat it, the people say, "From his hunger."

18 O my son! be content with thy daily bread and thy goods, and covet not what is another's.

19 O my son! be not neighbour to the fool, and eat not bread with him, and rejoice not in the calamities of thy neighbours.[1] If thine enemy wrong thee, show him kindness.

20 O my son! a man who fears God do thou fear him and honour him.

21 O my son! the ignorant man falls and stumbles, and the wise man, even if he stumbles, he is not shaken, and even if he falls he gets up quickly, and if he is sick, he can take care of his life. But as for the ignorant, stupid man, for his disease there is no drug.

22 O my son! if a man approach thee who is inferior to thyself, go forward to meet him, and remain standing, and if he cannot recompense thee, his Lord will recompense thee for him.

---

[1] Cf. Psalms CXLI. 4.

23 O my son! spare not to beat thy son, for the drubbing of thy son is like manure to the garden, and like tying the mouth of a purse, and like the tethering of beasts, and like the bolting of the door.

24 O my son! restrain thy son from wickedness, and teach him manners before he rebels against thee and brings thee into contempt amongst the people and thou hang thy head in the streets and the assemblies and thou be punished for the evil of his wicked deeds.

25 O my son! get thee a fat ox with a foreskin, and an ass great with its hoofs, and get not an ox with large horns, nor make friends with a tricky man, nor get a quarrelsome slave, nor a thievish handmaid, for everything which thou committest to them they will ruin.

26 O my son! let not thy parents curse thee, and the Lord be pleased with them; for it hath been said, "He who despiseth his father or his mother let him die the death (I mean the death of sin); and he who honoureth his parents shall prolong his days and his life and shall see all that is good."

27 O my son! walk not on the road without weapons, for thou knowest not when the foe may meet thee, so that thou mayst be ready for him.

28 O my son! be not like a bare, leafless tree that doth not grow, but be like a tree covered with its leaves and its boughs; for the man who has neither wife nor children is disgraced in the world and is hated by them, like a leafless and fruitless tree.

29 O my son! be like a fruitful tree on the roadside, whose fruit is eaten by all who pass by, and the beasts of the desert rest under its shade and eat of its leaves.

30 O my son! every sheep that wanders from its path and its companions becomes food for the wolf.

31 O my son! say not, 'My lord is a fool and I am wise," and relate not the speech of ignorance and folly, lest thou be despised by him.

32 O my son! be not one of those servants, to whom their lords say, "Get away from us," but be one of those to whom they say, "Approach and come near to us."

33 O my son! caress not thy slave in the presence of his companion, for thou knowest not which of them shall be of most value to thee in the end.

34 O my son! be not afraid of thy Lord who created thee, lest He be silent to thee.

35 O my son! make thy speech fair and sweeten thy tongue; and permit not thy companion to tread on thy foot, lest he tread at another time on thy breast.

36 O my son! if thou beat a wise man with a word of wisdom, it will lurk in his breast like a subtle sense of shame; but if thou drub the ignorant with a stick he will neither understand nor hear.

37 O my son! if thou send a wise man for thy needs, do not give him many orders, for he will do thy business as thou desirest: and if

thou send a fool, do not order him, but go thyself and do thy business, for if thou order him, he will not do what thou desirest. If they send thee on business, hasten to fulfil it quickly.

38 O my son! make not an enemy of a man stronger than thyself, for he will take thy measure, and his revenge on thee.

39 O my son! make trial of thy son, and of thy servant, before thou committest thy belongings to them, lest they make away with them; for he who hath a full hand is called wise, even if he be stupid and ignorant, and he who hath an empty hand is called poor, ignorant, even if he be the prince of sages.

40 O my son! I have eaten a colocynth, and swallowed aloes, and I have found nothing more bitter than poverty and scarcity.

41 O my son! teach thy son frugality and hunger, that he may do well in the management of his household.

42 O my son! teach not to the ignorant the language of wise men, for it will be burdensome to him.

43 O my son! display not thy condition to thy friend, lest thou be despised by him.

44 O my son! the blindness of the heart is more grievous than the blindness of the eyes, for the blindness of the eyes may be guided little by little, but the blindness of the heart is not guided, and it leaves the straight path, and goes in a crooked way.

45 O my son! the stumbling of a man with his foot is better than the stumbling of a n with his tongue.

46 O my son! a friend who is near is better than a more excellent brother who is far away.

47 O my son! beauty fades but learning lasts, and the world wanes and becomes vain, but a good name neither becomes vain nor wanes.

48 O my son! the man who hath no rest, his death were better than his life; and the sound of weeping is better than the sound of singing; for sorrow and weeping, if the fear of God be in them, are better than the sound of singing and rejoicing.

49 O my child! the thigh of a frog in thy hand is better than a goose in the pot of thy neighbour; and a sheep near thee is better than an ox far away; and a sparrow in thy hand is better than a thousand sparrows flying;[2] and poverty which gathers is better than the scattering of much provision; and a living fox is better than a dead lion; and a pound of wool is better than a pound of wealth, I mean of gold and silver; for the gold and the silver are hidden and covered up in the earth, and are not seen; but the wool stays in the markets and it is seen, and it is a beauty to him who wears it.

50 O my son! a small fortune is better than a scattered fortune.

51 O my son! a living dog is better than a dead poor man.

52 O my son! a poor man who does right is better than a rich man who is dead in sins.

---

[2] Cf. "A bird in the hand is worth two in the bush."

53 O my son! keep a word in thy heart, and it shall be much to thee, and beware lost thou reveal the secret of thy friend.

54 O my son! let not a word issue from thy mouth till thou hast taken counsel with thy heart. And stand not betwixt persons quarrelling, because from a bad word there comes a quarrel, and from a quarrel there comes war, and from war there comes fighting, and thou wilt be forced to bear witness; but run from thence and rest thyself.

55 O my son! withstand not a man stronger than thyself, but get thee a patient spirit, and endurance and an upright conduct, for there is nothing more excellent than that.

56 O my son! hate not thy first friend, for the second one may not last.

57 O my son! visit the poor in his affliction, and speak of him in the Sultan's presence, and do thy diligence to save him from the mouth of the lion.[3]

58 O my son! rejoice not in the death of thine enemy, for after a little while thou shalt be his neighbour, and him who mocks thee do thou respect and honour and be beforehand with him in greeting.

59 O my son! if water would stand still in heaven, and a black crow become white, and myrrh grow sweet as honey, then ignorant men and fools might understand and become wise.

---

[3] Cf. 2 Timothy, IV, 17.

60 O my son! if thou desire to be wise, restrain thy tongue from lying, and thy hand from stealing, and thine eyes from beholding evil; then thou wilt be called wise.

61 O my son! let the wise man beat thee with a rod, but let not the fool anoint thee with sweet salve. Be humble in thy youth and thou shalt be honoured in thine old age.

62 O my son! withstand not a man in the days of his power, nor a river in the days of its flood.

63 O my son! be not hasty in the wedding of a wife, for if it turns out well, she will say, 'My lord, make provision for me'; and if it turns out ill, she will rate at him who was the cause of it.

64 O my son! whosoever is elegant in his dress, he is the same in his speech; and he who has a mean appearance in his dress, he also is the same in his speech.

65 O my son! if thou hast committed a theft, make it known to the Sultan, and give him a share of it, that thou mayst be delivered from him, for otherwise thou wilt endure bitterness.

66 O my son! make a friend of the man whose hand is satisfied and filled, and make no friend of the man whose hand is closed and hungry.

67 There are four things in which neither the king nor his army can be secure: oppression by the vizier, and bad government, and perversion of the will, and tyranny over the subject; and four things which cannot be hidden: the prudent, and the foolish, and the rich, and the poor.'

CHAPTER III

Ahikar retires from active participation in affairs of state. He turns over his possessions to his treacherous nephew. Here is the amazing story of how a thankless profligate turns forgerer. A clever plot to entangle Ahikar results in his being condemned to death. Apparently the end of Ahikar.

Thus spake Haiqâr, and when he had finished these injunctions and proverbs to Nadan, his sister's son, he imagined that he would keep them all, and he knew not that instead of that he was displaying to him weariness and contempt and mockery.

2 Thereafter Haiqâr sat still in his house and delivered over to Nadan all his goods, and the slaves, and the handmaidens, and the horses, and the cattle, and everything else that he had possessed and gained; and the power of bidding and of forbidding remained in the hand of Nadan.

3 And Haiqâr sat at rest in his house, and every now and then Haiqâr went and paid his respects to the king, and returned home.

4 Now when Nadan perceived that the power of bidding and of forbidding was in his own hand, he despised the position of Haiqâr and scoffed at him, and set about blaming him whenever he appeared, saying, 'My uncle Haiqâr is in his dotage, and he knows nothing now.'

5 And he began to beat the slaves and the handmaidens, and to sell the horses and the camels and be spendthrift with all that his uncle Haiqâr had owned.

6 And when Haiqâr saw that he had no compassion on his servants nor on his household, he arose and chased him from his house, and sent to inform the king that he had scattered his possessions and his provision.

7 And the king arose and called Nadan and said to him: 'Whilst Haiqâr remains in health, no one shall rule over his goods, nor over his household, nor over his possessions.'

8 And the hand of Nadan was lifted off from his uncle Haiqâr and from all his goods, and in the meantime he went neither in nor out, nor did he greet him.

9 Thereupon Haiqâr repented him of his toil with Nadan his sister's son, and he continued to be very sorrowful.

10 And Nadan had a younger brother named Benuzârdân, so Haiqâr took him to himself in place of Nadan, and brought up and honoured him with the utmost honour. And he delivered over to him all that he possessed, and made him governor of his house.

11 Now when Nadan perceived what had happened he was seized with envy and jealousy, and he began to complain to every one who questioned him, and to mock his, uncle Haiqâr, saying: 'My uncle has chased me from his house, and has preferred my brother to me, but if the Most High God give me the power, I shall bring upon him the misfortune of being killed.'

12 And Nadan continued to meditate as to the stumbling-block he might contrive for him. And after a while Nadan turned it over in his mind, and wrote a letter to Achish, son of Shah the Wise, king of Persia, saying thus:

13 'Peace and health and might and honour from Sennacherib king of Assyria and Nineveh, and from his vizier and his secretary Haiqâr unto thee, O great king! Let there be pence between thee and me.

14 And when this letter reaches thee, if thou wilt arise and go quickly to the plain of Nisrîn, and to Assyria, and Nineveh, I will deliver up the kingdom to thee without war and without battle-array.'

15 And he wrote also another letter in the name of Haiqâr to Pharaoh king of Egypt. 'Let there be peace between thee and me, O mighty king!

16 If at the time of this letter reaching thee thou wilt arise and go to Assyria and Nineveh to the plain of Nisrîn, I will deliver up to thee the kingdom without war and without fighting.'

17 And the writing of Nadan was like to the writing of his uncle Haiqâr.

18 Then he folded the two letters, and sealed them with the seal of his uncle Haiqâr; they were nevertheless in the king's palace.

19 Then he went and wrote a letter likewise from the king to his uncle Haiqâr: 'Peace and health to my Vizier, my Secretary, my Chancellor, Haiqâr.

20 O Haiqâr, when this letter reaches thee, assemble all the soldiers who are with thee, and let them be perfect in clothing and

in numbers, and bring them to me on the fifth day in the plain of Nisrîn.

21 And when thou shalt see me there coming towards thee, haste and make the army move against me as an enemy who would fight with me, for I have with me the ambassadors of Pharaoh king of Egypt, that they may see the strength of our army and may fear us, for they are our enemies and they hate us.'

22 Then he sealed the letter and sent it to Haiqâr by one of the king's servants. And he took the other letter which he had written and spread it before the king and read it to him and showed him the seal.

23 And when the king heard what was in the letter he was perplexed with a great perplexity and was wroth with a great and fierce wrath, and said, 'Ah, I have shown my wisdom! what have I done to Haiqâr that he has written these letters to my enemies? Is this my recompense from him for my benefits to him?'

24 And Nadan said to him, 'Be not grieved, O king! nor be wroth, but let us go to the plain of Nisrîn and see if the tale be true or not.'

25 Then Nadan arose on the fifth day and took the king and the soldiers and the vizier, and they went to the desert to the plain of Nisrîn. And the king looked, and lo! Haiqâr and the army were set in array.

26 And when Haiqâr saw that the king was there, he approached and signalled to the army to move as in war and to fight in array

against the king as it had been found in the letter, he not knowing what a pit Nadan had digged for him.

27 And when the king saw the act of Haiqâr he was seized with anxiety and terror and perplexity, and was wroth with a great wrath.

28 And Nadan said to him, 'Hast thou seen, O my lord the king! what this wretch has done? but be not thou wroth and be not grieved nor pained, but go to thy house and sit on thy throne, and I will bring Haiqâr to thee bound and chained with chains, and I will chase away thine enemy from thee without toil.'

29 And the king returned to his throne, being provoked about Haiqâr, and did nothing concerning him. And Nadan went to Haiqâr and said to him, 'W'allah, O my uncle! The king verily rejoiceth in thee with great joy and thanks thee for having done what he commanded thee.

30 And now he hath sent me to thee that thou mayst dismiss the soldiers to their duties and come thyself to him with thy hands bound behind thee, and thy feet chained, that the ambassadors of Pharaoh may see this, and that the king may be feared by them and by their king.'

31 Then answered Haiqâr and said, 'To hear is to obey.' And he arose straightway and bound his hands behind him, and chained his feet.

32 And Nadan took him and went with him to the king. And when Haiqâr entered the king's presence he did obeisance before him on the ground, and wished for power and perpetual life to the king.

33 Then said the king, 'O Haiqâr, my Secretary, the Governor of my affairs, my Chancellor, the ruler of my State, tell me what evil have I done to thee that thou hast rewarded me by this ugly deed.'

34 Then they showed him the letters in his writing and with his seal. And when Haiqâr saw this, his limbs trembled and his tongue was tied at once, and he was unable to speak a word from fear; but he hung his head towards the earth and was dumb.

35 And when the king saw this, he felt certain that the thing was from him, and he straightway arose and commanded them to kill Haiqâr, and to strike his neck with the sword outside of the city.

36 Then Nadan screamed and said, 'O Haiqâr, O blackface! what avails thee thy meditation or thy power in the doing of this deed to the king?'

37 Thus says the story-teller. And the name of the swordsman was Abu Samîk. And the king said to him, 'O swordsman! arise, go, cleave the neck of Haiqâr at the door of his house, and cast away his head from his body a hundred cubits.'

38 Then Haiqâr knelt before the king, and said, 'Let my lord the king live for ever! and if thou desire to slay me, let thy wish be fulfilled; and I know that I am not guilty, but the wicked man bas to give an account of his wickedness; nevertheless, O my lord the king! I beg of thee and of thy friendship, permit the swordsman to give my body to my slaves, that they may bury me, and let thy slave be thy sacrifice.'

39 The king arose and commanded the swordsman to do with him according to his desire.

40 And he straightway commanded his servants to take Haiqâr and the swordsman and go with him naked that they might slay him.

41 And when Haiqâr knew for certain that he was to be slain he sent to his wife, and said to her, 'Come out and meet me, and let there be with thee a thousand young virgins, and dress them in gowns of purple and silk that they may weep for me before my death.

42 And prepare a table for the swordsman and for his servants. And mingle plenty of wine, that they may drink.'

43 And she did all that he commanded her. And she was very wise, clever, and prudent. And she united all possible courtesy and learning.

44 And when the army of the king and the swordsman arrived the found the table set in order, and the wine and the luxurious viands, and they began eating and drinking till they were gorged and drunken.

45 Then Haiqâr took the swordsman aside apart from the company and said, 'O Abu Samîk, dost thou not know that when Sarhadum the king, the father of Sennacherib, wanted to kill thee, I took thee and hid thee in a certain place till the king's anger subsided and he asked for thee?

46 And when I brought thee into his presence he rejoiced in thee: and now remember the kindness I did thee.

47 And I know that the king will repent him about me and will be wroth with a great wrath about my execution.

48 For I am not guilty, and it shall be when thou shalt present me before him in his palace, thou shalt meet with great good fortune, and know that Nadan my sister's son has deceived me and has done this bad deed to me, and the king will repent of having slain me; and now I have a cellar in the garden of my house, and no one knows of it.

49 Hide me in it with the knowledge of my wife. And I have a slave in prison who deserves to be killed.

50 Bring him out and dress him in my clothes, and command the servants when they are drunk to slay him. They will not know who it is they are killing.

51 And cast away his head a hundred cubits from his body, and give his body to my slaves that they may bury it. And thou shalt have laid up a great treasure with me.

52 And then the swordsman did as Haiqâr had commanded him, and he went to the king and said to him, 'May thy head live for ever!'

53 Then Haiqâr's wife let down to him in the hiding-place every week what sufficed for him, and no one knew of it but herself.

54 And the story was reported and repeated and spread abroad in every place of how Haiqâr the Sage had been slain and was dead, and all the people of that city mourned for him.

55 And they wept and said: 'Alas for thee, O Haiqâr! and for thy learning and thy courtesy! How sad about thee and about thy knowledge! Where can another like thee be found? and where can there be a man so intelligent, so learned, so skilled in ruling as to resemble thee that he may fill thy place?'

56 But the king was repenting about Haiqâr, and his repentance availed him naught.

57 Then he called for Nadan and said to him, 'Go and take thy friends with thee and make a mourning and a weeping for thy uncle Haiqâr, and lament for him as the custom is, doing honour to his memory.'

58 But when Nadan, the foolish, the ignorant, the hardhearted, went to the house of his uncle, he neither wept nor sorrowed nor wailed, but assembled heartless and dissolute people and set about eating and drinking.[4]

59 And Nadan began to seize the maidservants and the slaves belonging to Haiqâr, and bound them and tortured them and drubbed them with a sore drubbing.

60 And he did not respect the wife of his uncle, she who had brought him up like her own boy, but wanted her to fall into sin with him.

---

[4] Compare this account of Nadan's revelry and his beating of the servants with Matthew XXIV. 48-51 and Luke XII. 43-46. You will see that the language of Ahikar has colored one of our Lord's parables.

61 But Haiqâr had been cut into the hiding-place, and he heard the weeping of his slaves and his neighbours, and he praised the Most High God, the Merciful One, and gave thanks, and he always prayed and besought the Most High God.

62 And the swordsman came from time to time to Haiqâr whilst he was in the midst of the hiding-place: and Haiqâr came and entreated him. And he comforted him and wished him deliverance.

63 And when the story was reported in other countries that Haiqâr the Sage had been slain, all the kings were grieved and despised king Sennacherib, and they lamented over Haiqâr the solver of riddles.

CHAPTER IV

"The Riddles of the Sphinx." What really happened to Ahikar. His return.

And when the king of Egypt had made sure that Haiqâr was slain, he arose straightway and wrote a letter to king Sennacherib, reminding him in it 'of the peace and the health and the might and the honour which we wish specially for thee, my beloved brother, king Sennacherib.

2 I have been desiring to build a castle between the heaven and the earth, and I want thee to send me a wise, clever man from thyself to build it for me, and to answer me all my questions, and that I may have the taxes and the custom duties of Assyria for three years.'

3 Then he sealed the letter and sent it to Sennacherib.

4 He took it and read it and gave it to his viziers and to the nobles of his kingdom, and they were perplexed and ashamed, and he was wroth with a great wrath, and was puzzled about how he should act.

5 Then he assembled the old men and the learned men and the wise men and the philosophers, and the diviners and the astrologers, and every one who was in his country, and read them the letter and said to them, 'Who amongst you will go to Pharaoh king of Egypt and answer him his questions?'

6 And they said to him, 'O our lord the king! know thou that there is none in thy kingdom who is acquainted with these questions except Haiqâr, thy vizier and secretary.

7 But as for us, we have no skill in this, unless it be Nadan, his sister's son, for he taught him all his wisdom and learning and knowledge. Call him to thee, perchance he may untie this hard knot.'

8 Then the king called Nadan and said to him, 'Look at this letter and understand what is in it.' And when Nadan read it, he said, 'O my lord! who is able to build a castle between the heaven and the earth?'

9 And when the king heard the speech of Nadan he sorrowed with a great and sore sorrow, and stepped down from his throne and sat in the ashes, and began to weep and wail over Haiqâr.

10 Saying, 'O my grief! O Haiqâr, who didst know the secrets and the riddles! woe is me for thee, O Haiqâr! O teacher of my country and ruler of my kingdom, where shall I find thy like? O Haiqâr, O teacher of my country, where shall I turn for thee? woe is me for thee! how did I destroy thee! and I listened to the talk of a stupid, ignorant boy without knowledge, without religion, without manliness.

11 Ah! and again Ah for myself! who can give thee to me just for once, or bring me word that Haiqâr is alive? and I would give him the half of my kingdom.

12 Whence is this to me? Ah, Haiqâr! that I might see thee just for once, that I might take my fill of gazing at thee, and delighting in thee.

13 Ah! O my grief for thee to all time! O Haiqâr, how have I killed thee! and I tarried not in thy case till I had seen the end of the matter.'

14 And the king went on weeping night and day. Now when the swordsman saw the wrath of the king and his sorrow for Haiqâr, his heart was softened towards him,, and he approached into his presence and said to him:

15 'O my lord! command thy servants to cut off my head.' Then said the king to him: 'Woe to thee, Abu Samîk, what is thy fault?'

16 And the swordsman said unto him, 'O my master! every slave who acts contrary to the word of his master is killed, and I have acted contrary to thy command.'

17 Then the king said unto him. 'Woe unto thee, O Abu Samîk, in what hast thou acted contrary to my command?'

18 And the swordsman said unto him, 'O my lord! thou didst command me to kill Haiqâr, and I knew that thou wouldst repent thee concerning him, and that he had been wronged, and I hid him in a certain place, and I killed one of his slaves, and he is now safe in the cistern, and if thou command me I will bring him to thee.'

19 And the king said unto him. 'Woe to thee, O Abu Samîk! thou hast mocked me and I am thy lord.'

20 And the swordsman said unto him, 'Nay, but by the life of thy head, O my lord! Haiqâr is safe and alive.'

21 And when the king heard that saying, he felt sure of the matter, and his head swam, and he fainted from joy, and he commanded them to bring Haiqâr.

22 And he said to the swordsman, 'O trusty servant! if thy speech be true, I would fain enrich thee, and exalt thy dignity above that of all thy friends.'

23 And the swordsman went along rejoicing till he came to Haiqâr's house. And he opened the door of the hiding-place, and went down and found Haiqâr sitting, praising God, and thanking Him.

24 And he shouted to him, saying, 'O Haiqâr, I bring the greatest of joy, and happiness, and delight!'

25 And Haiqâr said to him, 'What is the news, O Abu Samîk?' And he told him all about Pharaoh from the beginning to the end. Then he took him and went to the king.

26 And when the king looked at him, he saw him in a state of want, and that his hair had grown long like the wild beasts' and his nails like the claws of an eagle, and that his body was dirty with dust, and the colour of his face had changed and faded and was now like ashes.

27 And when the king saw him he sorrowed over him and rose at once and embraced him and kissed him, and wept over him and said: 'Praise be to God! who hath brought thee back to me.'

28 Then he consoled him and comforted him. And he stripped off his robe, and put it on the swordsman, and was very gracious to him, and gave him great wealth, and made Haiqâr rest.

29 Then said Haiqâr to the king, 'Let my lord the king live for ever! These be the deeds of the children of the world. I have reared me a palm-tree that I might lean on it, and it bent sideways, and threw me down.

30 But, O my Lord! since I have appeared fore thee, let not care oppress thee! And the king said to him: 'Blessed be God, who showed thee mercy, and knew that thou wast wronged, and saved thee and delivered thee from being slain.

31 But go to the warm bath, and shave thy head, and cut thy nails, and change thy clothes, and amuse thyself for the space of forty days, that thou mayst do good to thyself and improve thy condition and the colour of thy face may come back to thee.'

32 Then the king stripped off his costly robe, and put it on Haiqâr, and Haiqâr thanked God and did obeisance to the king, and departed to his dwelling glad and happy, praising the Most High God.

33 And the people of his household rejoiced with him, and his friends and every one who heard that he was alive rejoiced also.

40

CHAPTER V

The letter of the "riddles" is shown to Ahikar. The boys on the eagles. The first "airplane" ride. Off to Egypt. Ahikar, being a man of wisdom also has a sense of humor. (Verse 27).

And he did as the king commanded him, and took rest for forty days.

2 Then he dressed himself his gayest dress, and went riding to the king, with his slaves behind him and before him, rejoicing and delighted.

3 But when Nadan his sister's son perceived what was happening, fear took hold of him and terror, and he was perplexed, not knowing what to do.

4 And when Haiqâr saw it he entered into the king's presence and greeted him, and he returned the greeting, and made him sit down at his side, saying to him,

'O my darling Haiqâr! look at these letters which the, king of Egypt sent to us, after he had heard that thou wast slain.

5 They have provoked us and overcome us, and many of the people of our country have fled to Egypt for fear of the taxes that the king of Egypt has sent to demand from us.

6 Then Haiqâr took the letter and read it and understood its contents.

7 Then he said to the king. 'Be not wroth, O my lord! I will go to Egypt, and I will return the answers to Pharaoh, and I will display this letter to him, and I will reply to him about the taxes, and I will send back all those who have run away; and I will put thy enemies to shame with the help of the Most High God, and for the Happiness of thy kingdom.'

8 And when the king heard this speech from Haiqâr he rejoiced with a great joy, and his heart was expanded and he showed him favour.

9 And Haiqâr said to the king: 'Grant me a delay of forty days that I may consider this question and manage it.' And the king permitted this.

10 And Haiqâr went to his dwelling, and he commanded the huntsmen to capture two young eaglets for him, and they captured them and brought them to him: and he commanded the weavers of ropes to weave two cables of cotton for him, each of them two thousand cubits long, and he had the carpenters brought and ordered them to make two great boxes, and they did this.

11 Then he took two little lads, and spent every day sacrificing lambs and feeding the eagles and the boys, and making the boys ride on the backs of the eagles, and he bound them with a firm knot, and tied the cable to the feet of the eagles, and let them soar upwards little by little every day, to a distance of ten cubits, till they grew accustomed and were educated to it; and they rose all the length of the rope till they reached the sky; the boys being on their backs. Then he drew them to himself.

JOSEPH'S PREDICAMENT

12 And when Haiqâr saw that his desire was fulfilled he charged the boys that when they were borne aloft to the sky they were to shout, saying:

13 'Bring us clay and stone, that we may build a castle for king Pharaoh, for we are idle.'

14 And Haiqâr was never done training them and exercising them till they had reached the utmost possible point (of skill).

15 Then leaving them he went to the king and said to him, 'O my lord! the work is finished according to thy desire. Arise with me that I may show thee the wonder.'

16 So the king sprang up and sat with Haiqâr and went to a wide place and sent to bring the eagles and the boys, and Haiqâr tied them and let them off into the air all the length of the ropes, and they began to shout as he had taught them. Then he drew them to himself and put them in their places.

17 And the king and those who were with him wondered with a great wonder: and the king kissed Haiqâr between his eyes and said to him, 'Go in peace, O my beloved! O pride of my kingdom! to Egypt and answer the questions of Pharaoh and overcome him by the strength of the Most High God.'

18 Then he bade him farewell, and took his troops and his army and the young men and the eagles, and went towards the dwellings of Egypt; and when he had arrived, he turned towards the country of the king.

19 And when the people of Egypt knew that Sennacherib had sent a man of his Privy Council to talk with Pharaoh and to answer his questions, they carried the news to king Pharaoh, and he sent a party of his Privy Councillors to bring him before him.

20 And he came and entered into the presence of Pharaoh, and did obeisance to him as it is fitting to do to kings.

21 And he said to him: 'O my lord the king! Sennacherib the king hails thee with abundance of peace and might, and honour.

22 And he has sent me, who am one of his slaves, that I may answer thee thy questions, and may fulfil all thy desire: for thou hast sent to seek from my lord the king a man who will build thee a castle between the heaven and the earth.

23 And I by the help of the Most High God and thy noble favour and the power of my lord the king will build it for thee as thou desirest.

24 But, O my lord the king! what thou hast said in it about the taxes of Egypt for three years--now the stability of a kingdom is strict justice, and if thou winnest and my hand hath no skill in replying to thee, then my lord the king will send thee the taxes which thou hast mentioned.

25 And if I shall have answered thee in thy questions, it shall remain for thee to send whatever thou hast mentioned to my lord the king.'

26 And when Pharaoh heard that speech, he wondered and was perplexed by the freedom of his tongue and the pleasantness of his speech.

27 And king Pharaoh said to him, 'O man! what is thy name?' And he said, 'Thy servant is Abiqâm, and I a little ant of the ants of king Sennacherib.'

28 And Pharaoh said to him, 'Had thy lord no one of higher dignity than thee, that he has sent me a little ant to reply to me, and to converse with me?'

29 And Haiqâr said to him, 'O my lord the king! I would to God Most High that I may fulfil what is on thy mind, for God is with the weak that He may confound the strong.'

30 Then Pharaoh commanded that they should prepare a dwelling for Abiqâm and supply him with provender, meat, and drink, and all that he needed.

31 And when it was finished, three days afterwards Pharaoh clothed himself in purple and red and sat on his throne, and all his viziers and the magnates of his kingdom were standing with their hands crossed, their feet close together, and their heads bowed.

32 And Pharaoh sent to fetch Abiqâm, and when he was presented to him, he did obeisance before him, and kissed the ground in front of him.

33 And king Pharaoh said to him, 'O Abiqâm, whom am I like? and the nobles of my kingdom, to whom are they like?'

34 And Haiqâr said to him, 'O my lord the kin I thou art like the idol Bel, and the nobles of thy kingdom are like his servants.'

35 He said to him, 'Go, and come back hither to-morrow.' So Haiqâr went as king Pharaoh had commanded him.

36 And on the morrow Haiqâr went into the presence of Pharaoh, and did obeisance, and stood before the king. And

Pharaoh was dressed in a red colour, and the nobles were dressed in white.

37 And Pharaoh said to him 'O Abiqâm, whom am I like? and the nobles of my kingdom, to whom are they like?'

38 And Abiqâm said to him, 'O my lord! thou art like the sun, and thy servants are like its beams.' And Pharaoh said to him, 'Go to thy dwelling, and come hither to-morrow.'

39 Then Pharaoh commanded his Court to wear pure white, and Pharaoh was dressed like them and sat upon his throne, and he commanded them to fetch Haiqâr. And he entered and sat down before him.

40 And Pharaoh said to him, 'O Abiqâm, whom am I like? and my nobles, to whom are they like?'

41 And Abiqâm said to him, 'O my lord! thou art like the moon, and thy nobles are like the planets and the stars.' And Pharaoh said to him, 'Go, and to-morrow be thou here.'

42 Then Pharaoh commanded his servants to wear robes of various colours, and Pharaoh wore a red velvet dress, and sat on his throne, and commanded them to fetch Abiqâm. And he entered and did obeisance before him.

43 And he said, 'O Abiqâm, whom am I like? and my armies, to whom are they like?' And he said, 'O my lord! thou art like the month of April, and thy armies are like its flowers.'

44 And when the king heard it he rejoiced with a great joy and said, 'O Abiqâm! the first time thou didst compare me to the idol Bel, and my nobles to his servants.

45 And the second time thou didst compare me to the sun, and my nobles to the sunbeams.

46 And the third time thou didst compare me to the moon, and my nobles to the planets and the stars.

47 And the fourth time thou didst compare me to the month of April, and my nobles to its flowers. But now, O Abiqâm! tell me, thy lord, king Sennacherib, whom is he like? and his nobles, to whom are they like?'

48 And Haiqâr shouted with a loud voice and said: 'Be it far from me to make mention of my lord the king and thou seated on thy throne. But get up on thy feet that I may tell thee whom my lord the king is like and to whom his nobles are like.'

49 And Pharaoh was perplexed by the freedom of his tongue and his boldness in answering. Then Pharaoh arose from his throne, and stood before Haiqâr, and said to him, 'Tell me now, that I may perceive whom thy lord the king is like, and his nobles, to whom they are like.'

50 And Haiqâr said to him: 'My lord is the God of heaven, and his nobles are the lightnings and the thunder, and when he wills the winds blow and the rain falls.

51 And he commands the thunder, and it lightens and rains, and he holds the sun, and it gives not its light, and the moon and the stars, and they circle not.

52 And he commands the tempest, and it blows and the rain falls and it tramples on April and destroys its flowers and its houses.'

53 And when Pharaoh heard this speech, he was greatly perplexed and was wroth with a great wrath, and said to him: 'O man! tell me the truth, and let me know who thou really art.'

54 And he told him the truth. 'I am Haiqâr the scribe, greatest of the Privy Councillors of king Sennacherib, and I am his vizier and the Governor of his kingdom, and his Chancellor.'

55 And he said to him, 'Thou hast told the truth in this saying. But we have heard of Haiqâr, that king Sennacherib has slain him, yet thou dost seem to be alive and well.'

56 And Haiqâr said to him, 'Yes, so it was, but praise be to God, who knoweth what is hidden, for my lord the king commanded me to be killed, and he believed the word of profligate men, but the Lord delivered me, and blessed is he who trusteth in Him.'

57 And Pharaoh said to Haiqâr, 'Go, and to-morrow be thou here, and tell me a word that I have never heard from my nobles nor from the people of my kingdom and my country.'

CHAPTER VI

The ruse succeeds. Ahikar answers every question of Pharaoh. The boys on the eagles are the climax of the day. Wit, so rarely found in the ancient Scriptures, is revealed in Verses 34-45.

And Haiqâr went to his dwelling, and wrote a letter, saying in it on this wise:

2 From Sennacherib king of Assyria. and Nineveh to Pharaoh king of Egypt.

3 'Peace be to thee, O my brother! and what we make known to thee by this is that a brother has need of his brother, and kings of each other, and my hope from thee is that thou wouldst lend me nine hundred talents of gold, for I need it for the victualling of some of the soldiers, that, I may spend it upon them. And after a little while I will send it thee.'

4 Then he folded the letter, and presented it on the morrow to Pharaoh.

5 And when he saw it, he was perplexed and said to him, 'Verily I have never heard anything like this language from any one.'

6 Then Haiqâr said to him, 'Truly this is a debt which thou owest to my lord the king.'

7 And Pharaoh accepted this, saying, 'O Haiqâr, it is the like of thee who are honest in the service of kings.

51

8 Blessed be God who hath made thee perfect in wisdom and hath adorned thee with philosophy and knowledge.

9 And now, O Haiqâr, there remains what we desire from thee, that thou shouldst build as a castle between heaven and earth.'

10 Then said Haiqâr, 'To hear is to obey. I will build thee a castle according to thy wish and choice; but, O my lord I prepare us lime and stone and clay and workmen, and I have skilled builders who will build for thee as thou desirest.'

11 And the king prepared all that for him, and they went to a wide place; and Haiqâr and his boys came to it, and he took the eagles and the young men with him; and the king and all his nobles went and the whole city assembled, that they might see what Haiqâr would do.

12 Then Haiqâr let the eagles out of the boxes, and tied the young men on their backs, and tied the ropes to the eagles' feet, and let them go in the air. And they soared upwards, till they remained between heaven and earth.

13 And the boys began to shout, saying, 'Bring bricks, bring clay, that we may build the king's castle, for we are standing idle!'

14 And the crowd were astonished and perplexed, and they wondered. And the king and his nobles wondered.

15 And Haiqâr and his servants began to beat the workmen, and they shouted for the king's troops, saying to them, 'Bring to the skilled workmen what they want and do not hinder them from their work.'

16 And the king said to him, 'Thou art mad; who can bring anything up to that distance?'

17 And Haiqâr said to him, 'O my lord! how shall we build a castle in the air? and if my lord the king were here, he would have built several castles in a single day.'

18 And Pharaoh said to him, 'Go, O Haiqâr, to thy dwelling, and rest, for we have given up building the castle, and to-morrow come to me.'

19 Then Haiqâr went to his dwelling and on the morrow he appeared before Pharaoh. And Pharaoh said, 'O Haiqâr, what news is there of the horse of thy lord? for when he neighs in the country of Assyria and Nineveh, and our mares hear his voice, they cast their young.'

20 And when Haiqâr heard this speech he went and took a cat, and bound her and began to flog her with a violent flogging till the Egyptians heard it, and they went and told the king about it.

21 And Pharaoh sent to fetch Haiqâr, and said to him, 'O Haiqâr, wherefore dost thou flog thus and beat that dumb beast?'

22 And Haiqâr said to him, my lord the king! verily she has done an ugly deed to me, and has deserved this drubbing and flogging, for my lord king Sennacherib had given me a fine cock, and he had a strong true voice and knew the hours of the day and the night.

23 And the cat got up this very night and cut off its head and went away, and because of this deed I have treated her to this drubbing.'

24 And Pharaoh said to him, 'O Haiqâr, I see from all this that thou art growing old and art in thy dotage, for between Egypt and Nineveh there are sixty-eight parasangs, and how did she go this very night and cut off the head of thy cock and come back?'

25 And Haiqâr said to him, 'O my lord! if there were such a distance between Egypt and Nineveh how could thy mares hear when my lord the king's horse neighs and cast their young? and how could the voice of the horse reach to Egypt?'

26 And when Pharaoh heard that, he knew that Haiqâr had answered his questions.

27 And Pharaoh said, 'O Haiqâr, I want thee to make me ropes of the sea-sand.'

28 And Haiqâr said to him, "O my lord the king! order them to bring me a rope out of the treasury that I may make one like it.'

29 Then Haiqâr went to the back of the house, and bored holes in the rough shore of the sea, and took a handful of sand in his hand, sea-sand, and when the sun rose, and penetrated into the holes, he spread the sand in the sun till it became as if woven like ropes.

30 And Haiqâr said, 'Command thy servants to take these ropes, and whenever thou desirest it, I will weave thee some like them.'

31 And Pharaoh said, 'O Haiqâr, we have a millstone here and it has been broken and I want thee to sew it up.'

32 Then Haiqâr looked at it, and found another stone.

33 And he said to Pharaoh 'O my lord! I am a foreigner: and I have no tool for sewing.

34 But I want thee to command thy faithful shoemakers to cut awls from this stone, that I may sew that millstone.'

35 Then Pharaoh and all his nobles laughed. And he said, 'Blessed be the Most High God, who gave thee this wit and knowledge.'

36 And when Pharaoh saw that Haiqâr had overcome him, and returned him his answers, he at once became excited, and commanded them to collect for him three years' taxes, and to bring them to Haiqâr.

37 And he stripped off his robes and put them upon Haiqâr, and his soldiers, and his servants, and gave him the expenses of his journey.

38 And he said to him, 'Go in peace, O strength of his lord and pride of his Doctors! have any of the Sultans thy like? give my greetings to thy lord king Sennacherib, and say to him how we have sent him gifts, for kings are content with little.'

39 Then Haiqâr arose, and kissed king Pharaoh's hands and kissed the ground in front of him, and wished him strength and continuance, and abundance in his treasury, and said to him, 'O my

lord! I desire from thee that not one of our countrymen may remain in Egypt.'

40 And Pharaoh arose and sent heralds to proclaim in the streets of Egypt that not one of the people of Assyria or Nineveh should remain in the land of Egypt, but that they should go with Haiqâr.

41 Then Haiqâr went and took leave of king Pharaoh, and journeyed, seeking the land of Assyria and Nineveh; and he had some treasures and a great deal of wealth.

42 And when the news reached king Sennacherib that Haiqâr was coming, he went out to meet him and rejoiced over him exceedingly with great joy and embraced him and kissed him and said to him, 'Welcome home: O kinsman! my brother Haiqâr, the strength of my kingdom, and pride of my realm.

43 Ask what thou would'st have from me, even if thou desirest the half of my kingdom and of my possessions.'

44 Then said Haiqâr unto him, 'O my lord the king, live for ever! Show favour, O my lord the king! to Abu Samîk in my stead, for my life was in the hands of God and in his.'

45 Then said Sennacherib the king, 'Honour be to thee, O my beloved Haiqâr! I will make the station of Abu Samîk the swordsman higher than all my Privy Councillors and my favourites.'

46 Then the king began to ask him how he had got on with Pharaoh from his first arrival until he had come away from his presence, and how he had answered all his questions, and how he

had received the taxes from him, and the changes of raiment and the presents.

47 And Sennacherib the king rejoiced with a great joy, and said to Haiqâr, 'Take what thou wouldst fain have of this tribute, for it is all within the grasp of thy hand.'

48 And Haiqâr mid: 'Let the king live for ever! I desire naught but the safety of my lord the king and the continuance of his greatness.

49 O my lord! what can I do with wealth and its like? but if thou wilt show me favour, give me Nadan, my sister's son, that I may recompense him for what he has done to me, and grant me his blood and hold me guiltless of it.'

50 And Sennacherib the king said, 'Take him, I have given him to thee.' And Haiqâr took Nadan, his sister's son, and bound his hands with chains of iron, and took him to his dwelling, and put a heavy fetter on his feet, and tied it with a tight knot, and after binding him thus he cast him into a dark room, beside the retiring-place, and appointed Nebu-hal as sentinel over him to give him a loaf of bread and a little water every day.

CHAPTER VII

The parables of Ahikar in which he completes his nephews education. Striking similes. Ahikar calls the boy picturesque names. Here ends the story of Ahikar.

And whenever Haiqâr went in or out he scolded Nadan, his sister's son, saying to him wisely:

2 'O Nadan, my boy! I have done to thee all that is good and kind and thou hast rewarded me for it with what is ugly and bad and with killing.

3 'O my son! it is said in the proverbs: He who listeneth not with his ear, they will make him listen with the scruff of his neck.'

4 And Nadan said, 'For what cause art thou wroth with me?'

5 And Haiqâr said to him, 'Because I brought thee up, and taught thee, and gave thee honour and respect and made thee great, and reared thee with the best of breeding, and seated thee in my place that thou mightest be my heir in the world, and thou didst treat me with killing and didst repay me with my ruin.

6 But the Lord knew that I was wronged, and He saved me from the ware which thou hadst set for me, for the Lord healeth the broken hearts and hindereth the envious and the haughty.

7 O my boy! thou hast been to me like the scorpion which when it strikes on brass, pierces it.

8 O my boy! thou art like the gazelle who was eating the roots of the madder, and it add me to-day and to-morrow they will tan they hide in my roots."

9 O my boy! thou hast been to who saw his comrade naked in the chilly time of winter; and he took cold water and poured it on him.

10 O my boy! thou hast been to me like a man who took a stone, and threw it up to heaven to stone his Lord with it. And the stone did not hit, and did not reach high enough, but it became the cause of guilt and sin.

11 O my boy! if thou hadst honoured me and respected me and hadst listened to my words thou wouldst have been my heir and wouldst have reigned over my dominions.

12 O my son! know thou that if the tail of the dog or the pig were ten cubits long it would not approach to the worth of the horse's even if it were like silk.

13 O my boy! I thought that thou wouldst have been my heir at my death; and thou through thy envy and thy insolence didst desire to kill me. But the Lord delivered me from thy cunning.

14 O my son! thou hast been to me like a trap which was set up on the dunghill, and there came a sparrow and found the trap set up. And the sparrow said to the trap, "What doest thou here?" Said the trap, "I am praying here to God."

15 And the lark asked it also, "What is the piece of wood that thou holdest?" Said the trap, "That is a young oak-tree on which I lean at the time of prayer."

16 Said the lark: "And what is that thing in thy mouth?" Said the trap: "That is bread and victuals which I carry for all the hungry and the poor who come near to me."

17 Said the lark: "Now then may I come forward and eat, for I am hungry?" And the trap said to him, "Come forward." And the lark approached that it, might eat.

18 But the trap sprang up and seized the lark by its neck.

19 And the lark answered and said to the trap, "If that is thy bread for the hungry God accepteth not thine alms and thy kind deeds.

20 And if that is thy fasting and thy prayers, God accepteth from thee neither thy fast nor thy prayer, and God will not perfect what is good concerning thee."

21 O my boy! thou hast been to me (as) a lion who made friends with an ass, and the ass kept walking before the lion for a time; and one day the lion sprang upon the ass and ate it up.

22 O my boy! thou hast been to me like a weevil in the wheat, for it does no good to anything, but spoils the wheat and gnaws it.

23 O my boy! thou hast been like a man who sowed ten measures of wheat, and when it was harvest time, he arose and reaped it, and garnered it, and threshed it, and toiled over it to the

very utmost, and it turned out to be ten measures, and its master said to it: "O thou lazy thing! thou hast not grown and thou hast not shrunk."

24 O my boy! thou hast been to me like the partridge that had been thrown into the net, and she could not save herself, but she called out to the partridges, that she might cast them with herself into the net.

25 O my son! thou hast been to me like the dog that was cold and it went into the potter's house to get warm.

26 And when it had got warm, it began to bark at them, and they chased it out and beat it, that it might not bite them.

27 O my son! thou hast been to me like the pig who went into the hot bath with people of quality, and when it came out of the hot bath, it saw a filthy hole and it went down and wallowed in it.

28 O my son! thou hast been to me like the goat which joined its comrades on their way to the sacrifice, and it was unable to save itself.

29 O my boy! the dog which is not fed from its hunting becomes food for flies.

30 O my son! the hand which does not labour and plough and (which) is greedy and cunning shall be cut away from its shoulder.

31 O my son! the eye in which light is not seen, the ravens shall pick at it and pluck it out.

32 O my boy! thou hast been to me like a tree whose branches they were cutting, and it said to them, "If something of me were not in your hands, verily you would be unable to cut me."

33 O my boy! thou art like the cat to whom they said: "Leave off thieving till we make for thee a chain of gold and feed thee with sugar and almonds."

34 And she said, "I am not forgetful of the craft of my father and my mother."

35 O my son! thou hast been like the serpent riding on a thorn-bush when he was in the midst of a river, and a wolf saw them and said, "Mischief upon mischief, and let him who is more mischievous than they direct both of them."

36 And the serpent said to the wolf, "The lambs and the goats and the sheep which thou hast eaten all thy life, wilt thou return them to their fathers and to their parents or no?"

37 Said the wolf, "No." And the serpent said to him, "I think that after myself thou art the worst of us."

38 O my boy! I fed thee with good food and thou didst not feed me with dry bread.

39 O my boy! I gave thee sugared water to. drink and good syrup, and thou didst not give me water from the well to drink.

40 O my boy! I taught thee, and brought thee up, and thou didst dig a hiding-place for me and didst conceal me.

41 O my boy! I brought thee up with the best upbringing and trained thee like a tall cedar; and thou hast twisted and bent me.

42 O my boy! it was my hope concerning thee that thou wouldst build me a fortified castle, that I might be concealed from my enemies in it, and thou didst become to me like one burying in the depth of the earth; but the Lord took pity on me and delivered me from thy cunning.

43 O my boy! I wished thee well, and thou didst reward me with evil and hatefulness, and now I would fain tear out thine eyes, and make thee food for dogs, and cut out thy tongue, and take off thy head with the edge of the sword, and recompense thee for thine abominable deeds.'

44 And when Nadan heard this speech from his uncle Haiqâr, he said: 'O my uncle! deal with me according to thy knowledge, and forgive me my sins, for who is there who hath sinned like me, or who is there who forgives like thee?

45 Accept me, O my uncle! Now I will serve in thy house, and groom thy horses and sweep up the dung of thy cattle, and feed thy sheep, for I am the wicked and thou art the righteous: I the guilty and thou the forgiving.'[5]

46 And Haiqâr said to him, 'O my boy! thou art like the tree which was fruitless beside the water, and its master was fain to cut it down, and it said to him, "Remove me to another place, and if I do not bear fruit, cut me down."

---

[5] Compare the parable of the Prodigal Son in Luke XV. 19.

47 And its master said to it, "Thou being beside the water hast not borne fruit, how shalt thou bear fruit when thou art in another place?"

48 O my boy! the old age of the eagle is better than the youth of the crow.

49 O my boy! they said to the wolf, "Keep away from the sheep lest their dust should harm thee." And the wolf said, "The dregs of the sheep's milk are good for my eyes."

50 O my boy! they made the wolf go to school that he might learn to read and they said to him, "Say A, B." He said, "Lamb and goat in my bell"

51 O my boy! they set the ass down at the table and he fell, and began to roll himself in the dust and one said, "Let him roll himself, for it is his nature, he will not change.

52 O my boy! the saying has been confirmed which runs: "If thou begettest a boy, call him thy son, and if thou rearest a boy, call him thy slave."

53 O my boy! he who doeth good shall meet with good; and he who doeth evil shall meet with evil, for the Lord requiteth a man according to the measure of his work.

54 O my boy! what shall I say more to thee than these sayings? for the Lord knoweth what is hidden, and is acquainted with the mysteries and the secrets.

55 And He will requite thee and will judge, betwixt me and thee, and will recompense thee according to thy desert.',

56 And when Nadan heard that speech from his uncle Haiqâr, he swelled up immediately and became like a blown-out bladder.

57 And his limbs swelled and his legs and his feet and his side, and he was torn and his belly burst asunder and his entrails were scattered, and he perished, and died.

58 And his latter end was destruction, and he went to hell. For he who digs a pit for his brother shall fall into it; and he who sets up traps shall be caught in them.

59 This is what happened and (what) we found about the tale of Haiqâr, and praise be to God for ever. Amen, and peace.

60 This chronicle is finished with the help of God, may He be exalted! Amen, Amen, Amen.

www.ingramcontent.com/pod-product-compliance
Lightning Source LLC
LaVergne TN
LVHW041458070426
835507LV00009B/672